REVIVAL IN ME

7 Things You Need to Live a Lifestyle of Revival

Contents:

I want to dedicate this book to my father, Joseph Vidulich, who loved the Lord with all his heart and served Him faithfully. He went home to be with the Lord in 2018. My father always encouraged me to follow the call of God on my life.

FOREWORD:
By Evangelist Kofi Acheampong

Evangelist Michael Vidulich and I first met in Hawaii on a mission trip and have stayed friends ever since. I have been privileged to see him go from a newly saved Christian to a mighty man of God.

I believe this book will bless you tremendously, as it has blessed me. This book will help kindle your love and passion for the Lord and the things of God. Therefore, I want to encourage you to read it with an open heart, ready to receive all that God has for you.

Michael, thanks for writing this great book.

Your friend,
Kofi.

INTRODUCTION:
7 THINGS YOU NEED TO LIVE A LIFESTYLE OF REVIVAL

Revival brings miracles! Revival takes you out of a mundane life. Revival snaps you out of your routine. Revival fans your flame! Revival stirs your faith which pleases God.

I've heard of many GREAT revivals. I've been in many GREAT revivals. Some say: "Those were the past. We'll never have those kinds of meetings again." I say: "You're right, we are going to have GREATER meetings". I'm contending for REVIVAL because I know revival causes you to seek God. When you seek God, He rewards you.

Revival brings healing and freedom into the land. Revival separates those who are hungry from those who just want to "play church."

Some might say, "Mike, how do you know these things?" Because it was in a revival meeting that the power of God touched me. It was in a revival meeting where I was healed and set free. It was in a revival meeting where I cried out to God to do a miracle in my life, and He did. It was in a revival meeting where the Lord reminded me of what He called me to do at a young age.

This is why I believe revival is a lifestyle. This is why I believe revival is for you!

I pray that as you read this book, that same hunger and passion God gave me sparks in you. Allow the Lord to reveal to you the steps you need to take in your everyday life to live a lifestyle of revival.

CHAPTER 1:
ALL THINGS NEW

"Therefore if any man be in Christ, he is a new creature: old things are passed away; behold, all things are become new."
2 Corinthians 5:17 KJV

The number one thing you need for a personal revival is salvation. Revival brings salvation. Revival brings into remembrance what Jesus did for us many years ago on the cross. The Holy Spirit does something new in us in revival, making us a new creation.

I pray with people of all ages, and if they've never received Jesus before, I tell them that when you accept Jesus, the Bible says we're a new creation! All things have been made new!

I prayed with this young boy once who had never heard about Jesus before. As I began telling him about Jesus, he decided to give his heart to the Lord. After, I asked him why he had a cast on his leg. He told me he had torn his ACL. As he told me the story, I felt the anointing to pray for his leg to be healed. I said to him, "The Lord wants to heal you." He replied, "Oh yeah?"

I said, "Yes! Do you believe that?" And he looked at me and said, "Not really." So, I started explaining to him about divine healing. I didn't let his answer discourage me because I understand that faith comes from hearing the Word of God. So that's what I began speaking. "You know, the Bible says all things have been made new, so according to the Bible, your leg can be made new." After seeing his faith grow, I asked him if he believed God could heal him. This time he said, "Yes, I do believe God can heal me."

Just taking a moment to explain to him what the Bible says and what God could do in his life changed his whole demeanor. After I prayed for him, he said, "I felt something! I felt like heat on my body!" I knew that was the anointing. I had felt in my spirit to tell him to remove his cast. In the natural, you can feel crazy when directing someone to do something radical, but I had to act in obedience to what I felt the Lord tell me to do. "Take that cast off," I said, "And do something you couldn't do before." He ripped his cast off, and his face turned white like a ghost! "I couldn't do this before." as he was bending his leg up and down. "I'm healed!" he said. I replied, "Jesus healed you! All things have been made new!"

Once you give your life over to the Lord, all things have been made new. You get a brand-new heart! A brand-new mind. Your spirit-man becomes activated. Maybe you're reading this saying, "Well, I've been a Christian, and salvation isn't new to me." Take yourself out of that "familiar" mindset. Don't think about things as "That's just how it's always been, and that's just how things will always be!"

"Remember ye not the former things, neither consider the things of old. Behold, I will do a new thing; now it shall spring forth; shall ye not know it? I will even make a way in the wilderness, and rivers in the desert."
Isaiah 43:18-19 KJV

Maybe you haven't received your healing, miracle, or breakthrough yet. I'm going to tell you to forget the former things. Today is a new day! Don't expect to read the Word of the Lord and not receive something. Do not have a mentality that says God isn't in the business of making all things new. If you got hurt in church, forget about it. Just forget about it. Today is a new day. Believe it or not, you can miss your breakthrough with that mentality. The "I've been to church before." "I've had hands laid on me, and nothing ever happened." It's time to change your confession and forget about that old way of thinking!

This is a brand-new day. God is doing new things. Are you expecting something new? Write down what you're expecting God to do! Expect God to do a miracle in your life. God does not change His ways. God does not change His thinking. God honors those who honor Him. If He did it before, He can do it again. If He did it for someone else, He can do it for you!

"Don't copy the behavior and customs of this world, but let God transform you into a new person by changing the way you think. Then you will learn to know God's will for you, which is good and pleasing and perfect."
Romans 12:2 NLT

"For there is no respect of persons with God."
Romans 2:11 KJV

What God does for others, He will also do for you. Too many times, people get caught up in comparison or jealousy over what God is doing in someone else's life. When you understand Romans 2:11, you celebrate others' victories because you know yours is coming. You become encouraged by others' testimonies because you know God will do the same thing for you!

"History merely repeats itself. It has all been done before. Nothing under the sun is truly new."
Ecclesiastes 1:9 NLT

If you're thinking, "Oh, I've gone too far for God to forgive me, or to use me, or to anoint me." You haven't. God will forgive you. God will redeem you. God will use you for His purpose. God will make all things new! He loves you. He wants you. God wants your heart. God wants your mind. God wants everything about you. Why? Because He is looking for the willing and obedient to bless and set you apart from the rest!

CHAPTER 2:
THE GIFT OF FAITH

"He alone is my rock and my salvation, my fortress
where I will never be shaken."
Psalms 62:2 NLT

Believing is being sold out. Believing means "I am not going to be moved. I'm not going to be afraid." Glory to God. Faith says, "You keep asking!" Faith says, "You keep seeking!" Faith says, "You keep knocking!" That's why I said in the beginning, if you're believing for your miracle, your healing, your breakthrough, then keep asking, keep seeking! Get hungry and ask the Holy Spirit, "What do I need to do to see my breakthrough?" He'll give you directions. He'll show you and tell you what you need to get done to have that manifested. Behold, God does new things.

"Keep on asking, and you will receive what you ask
for. Keep on seeking, and you will find. Keep on
knocking, and the door will be opened to you. For
everyone who asks, receives. Everyone who seeks,
finds. And to everyone who knocks, the door will be
opened."
Matthew 7:7-8 NLT

It takes faith to do that.

"Now faith is the substance of things hoped for, the evidence of things not seen."
Hebrews 11:1 KJV

Faith isn't natural. Faith is supernatural. So just because you don't see it in the natural doesn't mean it's not happening. Just because you don't see how that job will manifest, or you don't see your family will come to the Lord and be saved doesn't mean it's not happening. Just because you don't see that breakthrough doesn't mean it's not happening. It's happening by faith.

You might be reading this looking for direction in your life. Maybe you're tired of a mundane life. Perhaps you have decisions coming up, and you don't know what to do. You try to make sense of it in the natural. You make plans and write down everything, but you haven't received an answer. Maybe you have no peace. As you read this book, I pray that you'll get your answer from the Holy Spirit.

You come to God by faith. Faith is God's currency. When you do things by faith, you please God. When the gift of faith is in operation, you tap into the supernatural realm. God is not concerned about how big your problem is. He just wants you to have the faith to receive your answer. I heard a great man of God once say that it takes the same amount of faith to believe for one dollar that it does to believe for one million dollars.

"Dear brothers and sisters, when troubles of any kind come your way, consider it an opportunity for great joy. For you know that when your faith is tested, your endurance has a chance to grow."
James 1:2-3 NLT

Shortly after I had moved to Florida to go to Bible College, I had my truck "borrowed." I had a beautiful Cadillac Escalade. It was the last thing I owned from my business. I even used it to bring people to church when needed. To me, it wasn't "my" vehicle because I dedicated it to the Lord. I was just a steward of it. I would haul trailers for the ministry and offer to let them use the vehicle whenever needed. If there was a need, I was able to meet it. I like to live my life as a "need meeter." With help from the Holy Spirit, I meet people's needs. I'm blessed to do that.

A friend and I had just gotten back home in Tampa, FL, from traveling on the road with a ministry. My cousin was going to go to Bible college there, so I had picked up all her stuff in New York and brought it down in my Escalade. That Sunday morning, I was getting ready to go to church and came outside to find that someone "borrowed" my Escalade without asking. I went to my parking spot and thought, "That's... That's peculiar. My vehicle is not here."

I asked my friend who was with me, "Hey, we parked in the right spot, right? Maybe I got towed?" I called the tow company and found out they didn't have it.

Then it hit me, "Somebody borrowed my Escalade without asking! That's it." I called the police and filed a report. While doing this, something arose in my spirit. Faith came alive. I started operating in a gift of faith that I had not operated in before. I even told the police, "Someone borrowed my truck without asking me." She said, "Um. What do you mean? They stole it?" "No." I said, "Nobody steals anything from me because I don't allow people to steal from me. Somebody borrowed it." She said, "Okay, okay. That's interesting." I gave her my VIN, the model, the plate, everything. I mean, I'm in Tampa, Florida; how many Cadillac Escalades are driving around with a New York license plate? I said out loud, "By noon today, I'm going to get my Escalade back in Jesus' name." That took a mixture of faith to believe it and boldness to speak it.

I took an Uber to church. I want to make mention that even as I arrived to the church in an Uber, I didn't get out and run my mouth to my friends that someone "borrowed" my vehicle without asking. I watched what came out of my mouth. I didn't go looking for ten pastors to come into emergency prayer with me. I kept peace in my atmosphere and started praising the Lord for bringing my Escalade back. (James 1:2-3)

"Lord, I thank you that it's coming back. I call it by faith. I see it in the spirit, and I see my Escalade returning to me by noon in Jesus' name." I prayed. Again, I felt the gift of faith on me. Then, around 11:55 AM, my phone started ringing. "Hillsborough County police department, are you the owner of the Escalade? We found it."

I asked a friend to drive me to meet the officers who called. The entire time we were driving there, the devil was trying to lie to me, saying, "Well, you might have gotten your Escalade back, but it's going to be missing four tires, the radio, and all of your cousin's luggage is going to be gone, the things you had on it are all gone." I said quietly under my breath, "You stupid devil. No, it's not. My Escalade, along with everything in it, will be there. Nothing will be stolen from me in Jesus' name."

We pulled up to where my Escalade was abandoned. The police officer found it down the street from my apartment. It was even backed into the parking spot (just like I would have parked it). The cop said to me, "This is the weirdest thing. Not one thing looks to be bothered or stolen from your vehicle. Could you tell us if anything is missing?" I opened the back door, and all the luggage was there. I opened my door, and everything was there. All my money, cards, and license were there. Everything was left there, just the way I left it! The whole situation was "uncommon" in the natural. They broke into it, drove it down the block, and then abandoned it. They must have had such a conviction that the devils inside them couldn't even ride in peace.

I always share that story when I talk about faith because that day was when I encountered the gift of faith. I didn't go by what I saw in the natural but by what I saw in the spirit. I spoke it, and I believed it. Glory to God. The same thing can be for you. You can declare something by faith right now and you can see it come to pass. Maybe you're believing for a new job. Just keep speaking it. "I'm going to get a new job!" Perhaps you're believing for a new car. Say, "My car is going to be this color, style, and year!" Maybe you're believing for a new house. God is in the blessing business. God says in His Word that He is a rewarder of those who diligently seek Him. Seek His plan for your life.

"And it is impossible to please God without faith. Anyone who wants to come to him must believe that God exists and that he rewards those who sincerely seek him."
Hebrews 11:6 NLT

Keep your eyes on God, and do not let your mind get into fear or doubt. Instead, find out what His word says about your situation and stand on it! Don't allow the pressures and challenges of this world to change what God says. You are an overcomer!

Take a moment to speak out whatever it is you are believing God for to happen this year. Ask the Lord right now. Whether it's salvation for your family or you are believing for a financial miracle. Maybe you're believing for peace. Maybe you need direction. Perhaps it's an open door or a job. I pray that it will happen in Jesus' mighty name as you read this book.

Father, in the name of Jesus, we ask you right now for a miracle in our lives. We seek you right now for wisdom. We ask you right now for direction. Lord, I pray for unsaved loved ones and that they would receive salvation right now, and have an encounter with You. We invite you right now for miracles in the mighty name of Jesus. New body parts, new organs, new blood, and new thyroids. A new mind. Father, new hips, new joints. I'm asking you, Lord, for physical healing in their bodies right now. Lord, we ask you for a holy boldness according to your Word! In Jesus' mighty name. Amen.

CHAPTER 3:
ATMOSPHERE

"Enter into his gates with thanksgiving, and into his courts with praise: be thankful unto him, and bless his name."
Psalm 100:4 KJV

We have to develop an atmosphere around us where God is the center of it all. We must create an atmosphere of worship and thanksgiving. We must cultivate an attitude of praise. When you realize that you are in charge of your atmosphere, you take responsibility to create it. You realize that no one is going to praise Him for you. No one else is going to worship Him for you. No one else is going to give thanks to Him for you. You are responsible for your atmosphere, attitude, and confession.

You must come to God with an attitude of thanksgiving, not complaining and whining. Thanksgiving allows you to access God's presence. You are showing God gratitude by simply saying, "Lord. I thank you. If it weren't for you, I would not be here right now. If it weren't for you, I'd be broke, busted, and disgusted. I'd be somewhere lost, lonely, depressed. I thank you that Your Word holds power.

Your Word is truth. Your Word is alive. The plan that You've written down for me before I was even born is coming to pass." You could take the next 30 seconds and just say what you are grateful for. If you have a roof over your head and food in your fridge, thank Him for it!

Who you surround yourself with is essential. Who you associate with impacts your atmosphere. Who you spend time with and talk to the most tells me who you are.

"Don't be fooled by those who say such things, for "bad company corrupts good character."
1 Corinthians 15:33 NLT

If you're serious about feeding your faith, you need to hang around faith-like people. Have people in your life who aren't going to talk you out of God's plan for your life, but who are going to stand with you and encourage you.

The enemy wants to steal your hope. He wants to steal your future and tell you, "You're not going to make it. Just call it quits." That's what the enemy wants to do. That's why the atmosphere is so vital for a revival lifestyle. Think about it this way - if a doctor goes to do a procedure on somebody, they need to have the right atmosphere. Everything needs to be sanitary, right? Everything needs to be clean. They have to have the right tools. The Holy Spirit operates on people just like that. Sometimes, you can ask doctors, "Well, how long will this procedure take?" People start to do that to God when they get into His presence. Don't rush God. Allow the Holy Spirit to do the work, however long that takes. Don't be in a rush to get out of His presence.

When I first got saved, I had to develop an ear to hear God's voice. For me, it didn't happen instantly. First, I had to decide to get into the right atmosphere. I decided to go to church, win souls, tithe, give offerings, and seek after Him. Those are all decisions that you have to make, and those decisions will cause breakthrough to happen in your life. Decisions to obey God will open doors in your life. Decisions of getting into His Word and praying daily, hourly even, are all steps to creating the atmosphere for a personal revival.

"Come close to God, and God will come close to you…"
James 4:8 NLT

When you make up your mind to get into the right atmosphere and draw closer to God, He honors that. God is going to meet you where you are. He's not going to leave you nor forsake you. He's going to be with you to the end. Hallelujah.

"Yes, I am the vine; you are the branches. Those who remain in me, and I in them, will produce much fruit. For apart from me you can do nothing."
John 15:5 NLT

He's the vine, and I am the branch. The vine holds all the nutrients. Apart from God, we can do nothing. You have to get hungry for God. It's all up to you to put a demand on the anointing. Put a demand on the things of God. Take time to do that right now where you are.

CHAPTER 4:
YOU HAVE TO GET IN THE WORD

"For the word of God is alive and powerful. It is sharper than the sharpest two-edged sword, cutting between soul and spirit, between joint and marrow. It exposes our innermost thoughts and desires."
Hebrews 4:12 NLT

S ay that with me – "Alive and active, alive and not dormant. Not dead. Not unpowerful. Not mute. It's alive and active!" You need the Word. The Word gives life. Say it out loud: "The Word gives life!" The Word is important because you miss a massive key for a breakthrough without it.

"The Word of God is active right now.
In the beginning the Word already existed. The Word was with God, and the Word was God."
John 1:1 NLT

The Word is God. When you have the Word in you, you have God in you. Just like we read in James 1:2-3 when troubles, obstacles, and temptations come your way, you have the Word. A soldier is only as good as the weapons he carries, and the armor he has on.

Picture this: You're about to go into combat and your general says "Go into the armory and gear up." You're going to make sure you have full ammo, bullet-proof armor, and everything else you need.

God's Word is like a fully loaded weapon. His Word is protection. If you have His Word in you, you're locked and loaded. You're able to fight while maintaining peace. You're able to overcome while maintaining protected. The Word empowers you to resist the enemy.

"So humble yourselves before God. Resist the devil, and he will flee from you."
James 4:7 NLT

You can only resist the enemy through the authority God has already given you. Reading the Word of God reveals the power you have over the enemy.

"All Scripture is inspired by God and is useful to teach us what is true and to make us realize what is wrong in our lives. It corrects us when we are wrong and teaches us to do what is right."
2 Timothy 3:16 NLT

The Word empowers you to live holy. The Word will bring correction in your life. By studying and reading the Word, you are allowing yourself to become a disciple. That's why getting into the Word brings a personal revival. The Word changes you from the inside out. The Word reveals to you right and wrong. As you're reading this, I pray that a hunger will stir in you. Many times, people become frustrated feeling like their prayers aren't being answered, when the reality is they don't take time to read the Word.

"But if you remain in me and my words remain in you, you may ask for anything you want, and it will be granted!"
John 15:7 NLT

Getting into the Word of God is for our benefit. When you know the Word, you know what is accessible to you. You see the authority you carry. You understand the weight behind the words you confess.

God wants you to grow. God wants you to forgive. God wants to use you more than you want to be used. That's the truth. Unfortunately, when some people get to heaven, some will see the things God had for them to do here on earth, and they will see the other things they did instead. I pray that is not you. I pray that you will accomplish everything God has for you to do in Jesus' mighty name! The Holy Spirit will activate you to achieve heaven's goals for you.

"Thy word is a lamp unto my feet, and a light unto my path."
Psalm 119:105 KJV

Are you looking for direction in your life? Are you looking for guidance in a situation? Do you have a scripture you're standing on? Everything you need can be found in the Word of God. We hear people make foolish comments like, "Well, life doesn't come with a user manual." But that couldn't be further from the truth. Everything you could need guidance for is in the Bible.

"And be not conformed to this world: but be ye transformed by the renewing of your mind, that ye may prove what is that good, and acceptable, and perfect, will of God."
Romans 12:2 KJV

How do you renew your mind? By reading the Bible. You think different, walk different, and act different when you make it a daily priority to read the Word of God.

I challenge you to spend the next three weeks devoting 30 minutes a day to reading the Word of God. Start in the Book of John or Ephesians. I have never heard anyone say "I regret reading the Bible today"

"Study to shew thyself approved unto God, a workman that needeth not to be ashamed, rightly dividing the word of truth."
2 Timothy 2:15 KJV

CHAPTER 5:

YOU HAVE TO HAVE THE HOLY SPIRIT

"But when the Father sends the Advocate as my representative—that is, the Holy Spirit—he will teach you everything and will remind you of everything I have told you."
John 14:26 NLT

The Holy Spirit is the author of revival. The Holy Spirit is the one who revives us. He reveals Himself to us. The Holy Spirit empowers you to do what you are called to do.

However, some churches don't want the Holy Spirit because they don't want God to move. They don't want any changes. They don't want any disruptions. Some people don't want the Holy Spirit because He reveals things hidden in the dark.

The same Holy Spirit will teach you and give you knowledge and wisdom. He guides and convicts. The Holy Spirit leads and comforts. Having the Holy Spirit is a huge key to living a life of revival. He will stir up your gifts like no one else can.

The Holy Spirit will give you supernatural downloads. I'm not joking! He will speak to you. Some of you should just sleep with a pad and pen right next to your bed. Then, in the middle of the night, the Holy Spirit will speak to you and tell you things. It may just be one word, but on the other hand, He may give you an entire plan. He may even show you a picture.

I heard this incredible testimony from a man of God where the Holy Spirit showed him a picture of where his ministry building would be. He drew it out and had a real estate agent show them different properties. They went through all the properties until they found that exact picture! True story! They found a building that matched that drawing exactly! That's the Holy Spirit. Thank Him for those downloads right now.

The Holy Spirit also gives us boldness! If you allow Him to do the work in your life, He will change you from the inside out. He will provide you with the courage to become a witness to people.

"But you will receive power when the Holy Spirit has come upon you, and you will be my witnesses in Jerusalem and in all Judea and Samaria, and to the end of the earth."
Acts 1:8 NLT

This power that He talks about is the power to: 1) Live a holy life, free from sin. 2) Pull other people out of the darkness and into the light. 3) Create wealth and become a blessing. 4) Lay hands on the sick and watch them recover.

Another thing the Holy Spirit empowers you to do is pray with fervency. My wife and I talked about how we would pray for what felt like hours when we first got saved, but it had only been five minutes. Why was that? We hadn't built up our prayer life yet. We would just pray in tongues until we had the words to say. The Holy Spirit will pray God's perfect will through you when you don't know what to pray.

"And the Holy Spirit helps us in our weakness. For example, we don't know what God wants us to pray for. But the Holy Spirit prays for us with groanings that cannot be expressed in words."
Romans 8:26 NLT

Praying in tongues is a gift from the Holy Spirit. He will baptize you to speak in tongues if you allow Him.

"John answered their questions by saying, "I baptize you with water; but someone is coming soon who is greater than I am—so much greater that I'm not even worthy to be his slave and untie the straps of his sandals. He will baptize you with the Holy Spirit and with fire."
Luke 3:16 NLT

The Holy Spirit is a gentleman and will never force Himself on you. If you want to receive the gift of speaking in tongues, you can do that right now. Just pray this prayer:

"Jesus, I give you permission to baptize me with the Holy Spirit and fire, with evidence of speaking in tongues. I receive it in Jesus' name right now."

Just begin to allow Him to stir on the inside of you. He will give you the utterance, begin to open your mouth, and let the bubbling come out!

If you are already baptized in the Holy Spirit, take time right now to build up your spirit-man by speaking in tongues. Allow Him to reveal things to you as you do. Then, whatever He tells you to do, do it!

Constant quality time with the Holy Spirit is living a life of revival. Going where He wants you to go, doing what He wants you to do, and saying what He wants you to say.

CHAPTER 6:
YOU HAVE TO BE HUNGRY FOR GOD

"Blessed are they which do hunger and thirst after righteousness: for they shall be filled."
Matthew 5:6 KJV

The year was 2017. I remember starting my journey in ministry when God called me to go to Bible College. I was sitting in orientation class, and the whole time, I was thinking, "What am I doing here?" Then, during the next period, as orientation went on and the teachers were talking about what to expect in school, I remember feeling in my spirit the words "Stay hungry."

You see, when God called me to go to school for ministry, it was right after a radical encounter with Him. I knew that I knew I was on the right course. As people were speaking during orientation, they began to say, "Stay hungry, stay hungry." I even remember throughout the week meeting new students, and they would even tell me, "Just stay hungry."

Now, what exactly does that mean? Well, I'm going to tell you because hunger is a massive key for revival. Hunger means I'm going to do whatever it takes. I'm going to give whatever I need to give. I'm going to go wherever I need to go. I'm going to put the time in and put in the effort. I'm going to persevere for the things of God in my life.

In that year, I began to fast more than I ever fasted before. In that year, I was praying more in tongues. I had a decent-sized closet, and I remember putting a desk, a chair, a little light inside my closet. And I would go inside my closet and push all the clothes down to one side. And even in the middle of the night, when everyone was sleeping, I would be praying.

I'd be crying out to God, "Lord. I don't want to be an ordinary minister. I don't want to be an ordinary person. I want to see and do great things for you. I'll go where nobody else wants to go. I'll say what nobody else wants to say. I'll give what nobody else wants to give." It was hunger. It was a desperate call for God. I knew there were people that God would use me to reach. Some people would go to hell if it weren't for God using me to witness to them and to pray for them.

And that just came from being hungry. It's in a place of hunger where you can hear direction. My direction was to read and study. During this time in school, I would begin to read, study, and consecrate myself to what God had called me to do.

"But seek ye first the kingdom of God, and his righteousness; and all these things shall be added unto you."
Matthew 6:33 KJV

Hunger isn't just to have for Sunday morning. Hunger continues Monday, Tuesday, Wednesday, Thursday, Friday, Saturday, and back again on Sunday. To say that I'm hungry for God just one day a week doesn't cut it. You naturally eat every single day. Some people eat three times a day. Some people six or more times a day. You put a demand on the hunger.

How many times are you going to the throne room? How many times are you fellowshipping with God? Tell me your level of fellowship with God daily, and I'll tell you if you're really hungry. Do you acknowledge God in everything you do? Do you recognize God in the little things like driving to the coffee shop or driving to the food store? To be hungry is to be aware of His presence.

Begin to acknowledge Him throughout your day. Become sensitive to Him. Just like your body tells you to be mindful of hunger in the natural, allow your spirit-man to remind you of your desire for the things of God throughout your day. Never become satisfied with your spiritual growth. Always strive to go to the next level.

Where do you see yourself in the next year? What do you see yourself doing for the Kingdom of God? Are you a promoter of the Gospel? Are you someone who will fund the Kingdom? Are you someone who will populate heaven? Are you a creative for the Kingdom? Whatever it is: Your level of hunger will either accelerate you or slow you down. It will fuel you or drain you. You decide.

CHAPTER 7:
A REVIVAL LIFESTYLE IS A SOUL WINNING LIFESTYLE

"And he said unto them, Go ye into all the world,
and preach the gospel to every creature."
Mark 16:15 KJV

R evival produces soul winners. When you become so consumed with seeking after the things of God daily, you find out that the thing God cares most about is people. He wants everyone to know that He loves them and wants to have a relationship with them. That was the purpose of Jesus coming to earth.

"For God so loved the world, that he gave his only
begotten Son, that whosoever believeth in him should
not perish, but have everlasting life."
John 3:16 KJV

To contend for a revival lifestyle is to contend to see souls saved. The daily encounters with God result in daily opportunities to share His love with others. Like I said before, you become aware of God's presence in the coffee shop or the grocery store, and He shows you the assignment at hand. It is crucial not to ignore the

Holy Spirit when He highlights people to you. Obedience is key!

One Saturday morning in 2019, I remember waking up and feeling an urge to get the oil changed in my Escalade. I drove down that morning to a local body shop, a young man was behind the counter ringing me up. I felt impressed to start ministering to him and telling him that God loves him. Suddenly, a man came storming out of the backroom, pointing and yelling, "Where do you go to church!?"

I was a little taken back; I had never seen a reaction like that before. I told him the name of the church I went to, and he replied, "Well, I want to go to your church!" (I was very relieved to see where the conversation was going) It turns out he was the young man's father and owner of the body shop. He heard me sharing about the love of God and felt impressed to find out more.

That following day, he came to my church! I watched him during service to get an idea if he liked it or not. He showed little expression, and as we dismissed from service, he said, "I'll be back next week." I was so excited!

That man, my mechanic, went on to get saved, water baptized, plugged in, and brought his family to that church! To this day, he is still there serving God. It is so rewarding to see the transformation in his life. To think all of that happened because I felt the urge to get an oil change and was obedient to God to share the Gospel. Praise God!

God wants you to have these kinds of testimonies regularly. These testimonies shouldn't be "once in a lifetime" miracles. They should be everyday encounters! Who is in your path regularly that you could minister to and share the Gospel with? Maybe a local coffee barista, a waitress at your favorite restaurant, or perhaps your hairdresser? Every day people can get overlooked, but when you're sensitive to the Holy Spirit, He will highlight them to you.

> "But Samuel replied, "What is more pleasing to the Lord: your burnt offerings and sacrifices or your obedience to his voice? Listen! Obedience is better than sacrifice...""
> 1 Samuel 15:22 NLT

Remember that obedience is better than sacrifice when it comes to soul winning. We should never be discouraged or afraid when it comes to rejection. We aren't responsible for making someone get saved. We are responsible for providing them an opportunity to get saved.

"But how can they call on him to save them unless they believe in him? And how can they believe in him if they have never heard about him? And how can they hear about him unless someone tells them? 15 And how will anyone go and tell them without being sent? That is why the Scriptures say, "How beautiful are the feet of messengers who bring good news!""
Romans 10:14-15 NLT

This scripture isn't just for pastors or evangelists; it's for everyone! No matter your purpose on this earth, we are all called to share the Gospel. Whether you are called to ministry or not, we all have an assignment on this earth to reach people. Allow this to be you in Jesus' mighty name!

IS HEAVEN YOUR HOME?

If you're reading this book and find yourself feeling an urge to make things right with the Lord, I want to lead you through a simple prayer so you can be certain of your salvation.

"If you openly declare that Jesus is Lord and believe in your heart that God raised him from the dead, you will be saved."
Romans 10:9 NLT

If you would like to make Jesus Lord of your life today, say this prayer with your heart and your lips out loud:

"Dear Lord Jesus, come into my heart. Forgive me of my sins. Wash me and cleanse me. I believe you are the Son of God. I believe you died for me, rose from the dead, and that you are coming back for me. Fill me with Your Spirit. Give me a passion for the lost. Give me the ability to be all that you have created me to be. I'm saved, I'm born again, and I'm forgiven because I have Jesus in my heart. Amen!"

Whether you said that prayer for that first time or you just rededicated yourself back to Him, I want to say welcome to the Kingdom of God, my friend. You are as saved as I am. Serving the Lord is so rewarding!

ABOUT **MJV MINISTRIES**

"It's All About Souls!" More than a catchphrase, this is the Heavenly mandate and heartbeat of MJV Ministries. Michael and Sara Vidulich are Evangelists who have the heart to preach revival and see souls saved.

They travel to preach revival and train others to win souls in their everyday life. Evangelists Michael and Sara founded MJV Ministries in May of 2019. Since then, they have seen over 10,000 people accept Jesus into their hearts. Their passion is to reach the lost, feed the hungry, see the sick healed, and ignite revival everywhere they go.

To learn more about MJV Ministries, visit our website: mjvministries.com

READERS NOTES

READERS NOTES

READERS NOTES

READERS NOTES

revivalinme.com